I CAN'T DO IT... YET!

BLOOMSBURY EDUCATION

Bloomsbury Publishing Plc
50 Bedford Square, London WC1B 3DP, UK

Bloomsbury Publishing Ireland Limited
29 Earlsfort Terrace, Dublin 2, D02 AY28, Ireland

First published in Great Britain, 2026 by Bloomsbury Publishing Plc

A catalogue record for this book is available from the British Library

ISBN: PB: 9781801998031; ePub: 9781801998048

2 4 6 8 10 9 7 5 3 1

Printed and bound in China by C&C Offset Printing Co., Ltd., Shenzhen, Guangdong

To find out more about our authors and books visit www.bloomsbury.com and sign up for our newsletters

For product safety related questions contact productsafety@bloomsbury.com

I CAN'T DO IT... YET!

BLOOMSBURY EDUCATION
LONDON OXFORD NEW YORK NEW DELHI SYDNEY

From LONDON to JAMAICA...

...from MUMBAI to TIMBUKTU,

you will hear the same thing **SHOUTED**.
Can you guess it?
Need a clue?

You can hear it in the **jungle,**

in the **ocean**

and every **zoo.**

In your **school**

and on the **telly.**

Even **SHOUTED** from the **loo!**

Have you got it?
Do you know?

The thing we all shout
when we're learning to **GROW**...

I CAN'T

DO IT!

Frances the Cheetah
is learning to run,

but it's really not that easy
nor even that much fun.

I keep falling over, that's it!
I am done!

I CAN'T DO IT!

Agathe the Eagle and Maggie the Owl
are flying, frustrated, beginning to scowl.

Yet ANOTHER crash landing,
and now they both howl...
I CAN'T DO IT!

James the Bat has a bump on his head.
'Hanging upside down is hard,' he said.
'I'm giving up and sleeping in a bed.'

I CAN'T DO IT!

Nathan the Giraffe was walking really well,
then his knees turned to jelly and over he fell.
'I'm NEVER going to get this!' he said with a yell.

I CAN'T...

STOPP

PPP!!!!!!!!!!

'STOP!' screamed the mouse, now banging his gong!
'I've been trying to tell you, you've got it all wrong!
There's a word that's been missing the whole way along...

I can't do it... <u>YET!</u>'

A B C D E F G
It's normal to find things hard, you see.
2+2=?!
We all want to give up on tasks, even me.

But whenever you're struggling, please **DON'T** fret.
It's not that you **CAN'T** do it, you just can't do it **YET!**

'Whether you're learning to paint or trying to fly
there'll be times where you mess up and just want to **CRY**.
But that's when you **Stand tall** and shout to the sky...'

I CAN'T DO IT
YET!

Everyone was **excited**,
to learn they're allowed
to get things wrong along the way,
and still feel really **proud**.
Hehe!
Nearly!

They go back to their challenges but every night they phone,
to check in with each other so they know they're **not alone**.

As time goes by, through ups and downs
Our friends grow more each day.
Till one by one, they get to shout,

'I can do it now! HOORAY!'

So next time you are struggling or end up in a mess,

REMEMBER...

Set-backs are like treasure maps – they lead you to **success**!

I CAN'T DO

IT... YET!

WELCOME TO...

THE COURAGE CLUB

This story is part of **The Courage Club** series – helping children (and their adults!) build bravery, take risks, and go after hard things together.

The bigger picture

So much of our approach to mental health is reactive: we wait until there's a problem before stepping in to 'fix' it. At *The Courage Club* we believe in a more proactive approach - one that supports ALL children to build strong emotional foundations right from the start. This is not just to equip children with the tools to cope when life's challenges come but also to empower them with the skills to thrive well beyond that.

The Courage Club is built around three core strands of child development:

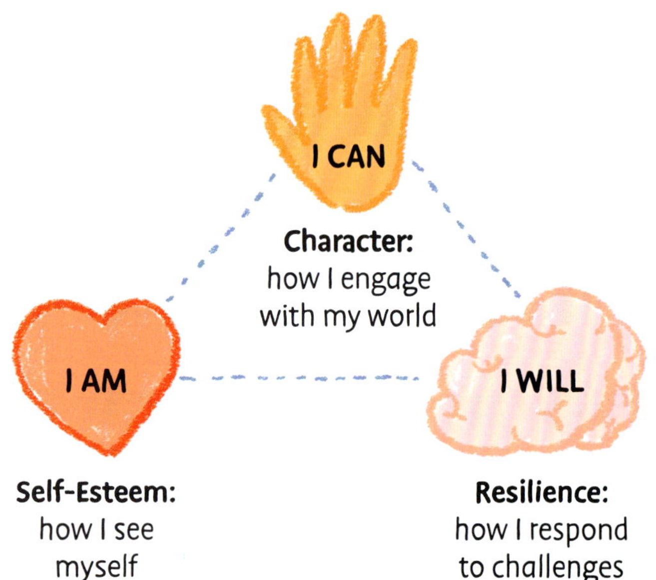

Where this story fits

I Can't Do it... Yet! helps children recognise that learning something new and making progress takes time. In a world that celebrates quick wins and short cuts, we want children to develop resilience to understand that hard things are worth doing and that perseverance matters more than instant success. When things are tough, adding the word YET makes all the difference. It tells children (and adults!) that struggle is not a sign to give up but rather A POWERFUL MESSAGE that you are ON THE RIGHT TRACK! When adults model this mindset, children begin to embody it for themselves.

So, let's keep saying it out loud, together: